CH00889972

POETIC VOYAGES SUFFOLK

Edited by Lucy Jeacock

First published in Great Britain in 2001 by
YOUNG WRITERS
Remus House,
Coltsfoot Drive,
Peterborough, PE2 9JX
Telephone (01733) 890066

All Rights Reserved

Copyright Contributors 2001

HB ISBN 0 75433 192 X
SB ISBN 0 75433 193 8

FOREWORD

Young Writers was established in 1991 with the aim to promote creative writing in children, to make reading and writing poetry fun.

This year once again, proved to be a tremendous success with over 88,000 entries received nationwide.

The Poetic Voyages competition has shown us the high standard of work and effort that children are capable of today. It is a reflection of the teaching skills in schools, the enthusiasm and creativity they have injected into their pupils shines clearly within this anthology.

The task of selecting poems was therefore a difficult one but nevertheless, an enjoyable experience. We hope you are as pleased with the final selection in *Poetic Voyages Suffolk* as we are.

CONTENTS

Holbrook Primary School

Ben Duff	20
Martyn Bass	20
Robert Carey	21
James Brown	22
Charlotte Gant	22
Rosanne Hiles	23
Matthew Parrish	24
James Loveland	25
Fabia Conington	26
Jessie Keeble	26
Thomas Stroud	27
Paul Barker	28
Matthew Longson	28
Poppy Fisk	29
Kate Barker	30
Charlotte Moore	31
Katie Milligan	31
Daniel Stebbings	32
Fiona Tunbridge	32
Theodore Vass	33
Mark Frost	34
Alex Christensen	34
Amy Swallow	35
Bethany Thrower	36
Stephanie Brazil	36

Hollesley Primary School

Zachary Powell	37
Rosie Daniell	37
Henry Kember	37
Rachel Pipe	38
Ryan Whitney	38
Sophie Sly	39
Amy Churchyard	39

Ipswich Preparatory School

Ellie Rogers	40
Rebecca Mulcahy	40
Hannah Jeffery	41
George Carlton-Brett	41
Ben Hills	42
Christian Swan	42
James Williams	43
Charlotte Robinson	44
Oliver Weller	45
George Rendall	46
Elizabeth McLachlan	46
Timmy Yung	47
Olivia Lewis	48
Alexander Mitchell	48
William Birkbeck-Martin	49
Joshua Godfrey	50
Iain Reynolds	50
Edward Messent	51
Ahrandeep Aujla	52
Ben Manning	53
Charles Davis	54

Martlesham Beacon Hill Primary School

Sophie Stokes	54
Jennifer Bickers	55
Abigail Savoy	55
Jennifer Thompson	56

Orwell Park School

Ivan Hunter Gordon	56
William Stott	57
Adnan Bashir	57
Lois Hunt	58
Heather Moate	59
Hugh Creasy	59
Edmund Compton	60

Georgia Grimmer	97
Victoria Turner	98
Harry Wing	98
Joseph Athorn	99
Gerard Gibson	100
Luke Clackett	101
Rachel Cooper	101
Lauren Hicks	102

Sir Robert Hitcham's CE Primary School

Rosa Forsdick-Hurr	102
Louise Perrier	103
Hannah Sewell	103
Sam Longstaff	104
Ruth Ellen Pintilie	104
Kerrie Ablitt	105
Sam Thurlow	105
Daniel Cable	106
Simon Pink	106
Michael Carruthers	107
Ria Turner	107
Bethany Scott	108
Emma Beard	108
Thomas Mann	109
Samantha Syrett	110
Lauren Wright	110
Robert Beavis	111
Luke Thompson	111
Charlotte Hammond	112
Bethany Chilvers	113
Rosie Webster	113
Hannah Tomlin	114
Sam Rowntree	115
Flora Mayo Jennings	116
Philip Mutton	116
Emily Mills	117

Weeting Primary School

Jessica Holder	136
Ellen Ferguson	136
Lucie Richardson	137
Aaron Markiewiecz	137
Duncan Hood	138
Gary Rickard	138
Alice Green	138
Shane Pueschel	139
Paul Barrett	139
Jordan Robinson	139
Claire Boggis	140
Sara Vine	140

The Poems

IN MY BOX:

In my box,

I have the sun
Snoring loudly,
Making the howl of the wind.

In my box,

I have the stars
Twinkling as if they are the
Smile of the universe.

In my box,

I have the moon
Circling round the
World every night.

In my box,

I have a comet,
Falling down from space,
In flames to the Earth.

In my box,

I have snow,
Falling gracefully,
From the sky,
Flaking as it goes
And sparkling in the winter sun.

My box is made of diamonds.
It has a gold snowflake keyhole.
It looks like a silver cloud,
Floating on my bookshelf.

Amy Jowett (10)
Bramford CE Primary School

GRAN'S LUNCH

When I go to Gran's, she's really cool,
We play bingo and swim in her pool!
But when she cooks, it's different you see,
She cooks loads of food, *and it's all for me!*

We'll start with the sprouts, well they're OK,
She cooks them until their colour is quite grey!
They are as hard as a rock, but who am I to complain?
You would break your teeth and end up in pain!

Her gravy is so lumpy, you eat it piece by piece,
Her gravy is so congealed, I wish her cooking would cease!
Her carrots are so soggy, they'll make you want to scream,
Her carrots are so mushy, you'll think you're in a bad dream!

Her cabbage is so ghastly, it's very, very slimy,
Her cabbage is revolting, and is very, very grimy!
So now you know, what my gran's cooking is like,
Please come round for lunch, it'll be alright!

Tom Wrigley (10)
Bramford CE Primary School

MY RIDDLE

My object is as crooked as an old man
It's bark is as smooth as silk.
In the winter months its hardy, bendy branches
                freeze in their shadows
My object has fruit, the colour of grass.

   What is it?

James Maguire (10)
Bramford CE Primary School

THE BOX

My box is dark and hard,
My box is starry and glittering,
My box has lightning striking from the sky,
When I step in my box there is a sandy hot beach,
When I step in my box there is a hot, blue calm sea,
When I step in my box there is a blazing sun
shining on palm trees,
When I step in my box there is a chocolate factory,
When I step in my box there is a last kiss from
a dying man,
When I step in my box there is an everlasting
hug from my mum.

Grace Hyam (10)
Bramford CE Primary School

FISH

The fish is brightly coloured: red, yellow and blue,
Swimming through the ocean with nothing else to do.

The fish is like a marble rolling in the sea,
Rolling towards you, so bright you can hardly see!

The fish is like a bright piece of paper swimming
in the glimmering sea.

Matthew Brown (10)
Bramford CE Primary School

THE MAGIC BOX

I will put in my box:

Bertie Bassett made of liquorice allsorts, all black and white
The eye of a snozzwanger blinking every five seconds,
And the tail of a scorpion using the eye to sting its enemy.

I will put in my box:

The sunrise moving slowly in the moonlit sky,
The transparent diamonds from a long-lost pirate glistening
                                    under the sunrise,
And a goblet of the finest wine drunk by Sir Braveheart.

I will put in my box:

The head of a Chinese dragon breathing fire and
                        tossing backwards and forwards,
A group of Spanish dancers opening and shutting their castanets
And the last kiss of a dying man.

I will put in my box:

Four shrivelled up roses starting to form nicely again
                        when the darkness disappears,
An ancient wizard chorusing a spell and waving a wand wildly,
And a roaring fire giving warmth to the bitter, cold air.

Danielle Eley (9)
Bramford CE Primary School

THE JUNGLE DIN!

Down in the deep, dark jungle,
Where snakes go *hissss!*
And parrots go squawk.

Pacing up and down,
Is the king of the jungle,
He roars louder than ever,
Making a roaring racket.

Everything goes quiet for a second,
Again the snakes go *hissss*
The parrots go squawk,
And the monkeys join in with a terrible laugh.

Still the lion paces up and down,
With a more serious look on his furry head,
The big cat roars and roars,
His mane looking as if it's going to blow away.

The animals stop at a jolt,
The monkeys run
The parrots jump
And the snakes slither.

Emma Williams (10)
Bramford CE Primary School

THE CRICKET MATCH

Number one,
Here he comes,
Goes to hit it,
Away from the wicket.

Number two,
With glamorous shoes,
Goes down on one knee,
And hits it straight past a tree.

Number three,
A good player was he,
Kept his eye on the ball,
And hit it over the wall.

Number four,
Was ever so poor,
His job is a builder,
He hit it straight to a fielder.

Number five,
Was late to arrive,
But he wasn't a winner,
Getting bowled by the spinner.

Number six,
Who was full of tricks,
With a swing, oh so grand
He hit it right over the stand.

The rest were no good,
They'd eaten too much pud,
And all had no luck,
As they were out for a duck.

It took a brilliant catch,
To finish the match!

David Scrutton (11)
Bucklesham Primary School

THE DREAMBOAT

The dreamboat gives out dreams,
Locked away in the hull,
It gives out exciting themes,
Not one is dull.
Without fail every night,
It sails across the evening sky,
To deliver dreams to children tucked up
tight,
The ship is disguised with a blue dye,
Over a million dreams to pick,
Matched to the right child,
The sailors move so quickly, they're extremely
carefully filed.
The dreamboat travels across the morning
sun,
Travelling to the land of the dream-makers.
For their day has just begun,
For they're the dream-rakers on the
dreamboat.

Anja Christensen (10)
Bucklesham Primary School

THE TIGER

Its warm tongue,
Its padded paws,
Its razor-sharp teeth,
Its outrageous claws.

The twilight is dismal,
The tiger is swift,
The speed and agility,
Like in a trance or drift.

He's like a hunter,
When it comes to chasing prey.
The animal's spirit is uplifted,
Throughout the day.

It's the eve of the day,
Now it's feasting time.
A time to relax
All the hunting and chasing
          was definitely worthwhile.

Lauren Attwood (10)
Bucklesham Primary School

VALENTINE'S DAY

Hearts and kisses on this romantic day,
Valentines are coming this way,
Cards and presents on this Valentine's Day,
How romantic in every way.
This romantic day comes once a year,
So make your intentions very clear.

Amy Creasey (10)
Bucklesham Primary School

THE CRUNCHY CAKE

George felt hungry so he said
'I know, I'll make a delicious cake.'
He poured in coffee and some chewy toffee,
in went pepper with a pinch of salt,
frogs' legs, chocolate, mushy beans,
ketchup and some mouldy peas.
In they slopped, beans and all,
the cake looked marvellous, the best one of all.
As George mixed and stirred with wonderful glee
his smile became bigger, as big as a '3'.
The cake looked too dark so he poured in mustard
it looked too sloppy, so in went custard.
George put it in the oven to bake
but then he realised he'd made a mistake.
The cake started to shrivel and burn to a crisp,
The smoke billowed out with a great loud *hisssss!*
The ceiling collapsed, the floor gave way
George screamed very loudly and ran away.

Anneliese King (10)
Bucklesham Primary School

????

I make you feel relaxed,
I am very comfy,
I move on my feet with a push,
You can sink right down in my tummy,
I'm as comfortable as a bed
And you use me when you've come
    home from a tiring day at work.

What am I?

Samantha Catling (10)
Bucklesham Primary School

THE TOAD

'What is your name?'
I asked a toad,
It didn't reply
It just sat on the road.

I waited and waited
But that toad just stared,
I heard a noise
But the toad wasn't scared.

Along came a lorry
With a big load,
And I felt quite sorry
Because it squashed that old toad.

Karina Scrutton (8)
Bucklesham Primary School

MY HORSE AND I

Clip-clop go the horse's feet
As we go along the street
Clip-clop goes the drum-like beat
We stopped and had a seat
In the glorious big sun's heat
I got back on
And we were gone
I feel as light as a feather
It really is the best feeling ever!

Grayling Marsh (8)
Bucklesham Primary School

RAINDROP VOYAGES

I'm starting my journey
   From up in the clouds

      I'm going to witness
      Breathtaking sights
      And amazing sounds . . .

Here I go into a stream, it   *like an*
      seems   *incredible,*
                colourful
                    dream,

I see a rainbow made by myself
         and a bright sunbeam.

Frances Edwards (10)
Colneis County Junior School

THE VOYAGE

While the sun is rising
high up in the sky
We are saying to the night
A sleepy bye bye.

The sun is at its highest
In the middle of the day
Wonderful shades of gold
Sending down powerful rays.

A black velvet blanket
Studded with glittering stars
Is thrown over the fading sun
And night has begun.

Hannah Rowe (9)
Colneis County Junior School

VIKING VOYAGE

Behind me, the sound of heavy footsteps.
Quick! Run!
Across fields,
Across meadows,
Through woods,
And onto the beach.
I turned around.
Where were the footsteps now?

I crouched, listening,
There they were again.
In the distance
Men with wild beards.,
Strange helmets and patterned shields.
Nervously, I licked my furry paw -
                    Vikings!
I ran until . . .
Safe at last.

'All aboard!'
Shouted a deep, muffled voice from the deck.
And with the noise of oars through water
And wild ideas in my head,
I knew,
I was to be,
The first, tabby, Viking Voyager.

Joshua Rayner (10)
Colneis County Junior School

THE LONESOME TRAVELLER

The winding tracks,
The dusty roads,
The dying sun,
No place called home.

The weary man
Goes on his way.
Through day and night.
Through night and day.

The burning sun,
Beats on his head,
No place to sleep,
No proper bed.

As he turns round,
Another bend,
He knows there is,
No final end.

He's in luck,
A barn's in sight,
A sheltered place to
Spend the night.

But he's never
There to stay.
He's off to start
Another day.

Miranda Overett (9)
Colneis County Junior School

BABY TO ELDERLY

Screaming baby, just been born
Wrapped up warm for his family to see,
How quickly he grew into a boy
Just started school and learning to read
His life is busy with clubs and fun,
Now he's an adult, his life has begun,
He's found the girl of his dream,
And he's made a family with children of his own.
He's got a job that pays a lot,
His life has gone fast, he's just turned *60*
His two grandchildren have been born and
He's just decided to retire!

> *Elderly person*
> *has been made!*

Emily Shevlin (10)
Colneis County Junior School

SUMMER'S DREAM

All tired I rest my weary head,
Upon my pillow in the bed,
My eyelids closed unable to peep,
I drift off now into a deep, deep sleep.

I find myself in a golden land,
Where ladies and fawns are hand-in-hand,
The sun shines on, and on and on,
This perfect day will never be gone.

I slowly turn and then I hear,
Not the sound of the small deer,
But a bell it would seem,
I'm awakening from this dream.

Kathryn Stone (9)
Colneis County Junior School

DREAMLAND

When everyone is snuggled up all warm inside their beds,
And dazzling sights and visions are whirling round
                          and round their heads,
And cats and dogs don't hear the silent mice, as they quietly tread,
I leave my home, and slowly fly to Dreamland.

I soar over tiny pin-like towns
And minute sailing ships
The fishermen stare in disbelief
And the watchman nearly trips.

Soon I come to my destination
A thrilling outside world
The air is sprayed with pretty colours
Into which spirals are curled.

But sadly, soon it will all be over
And I will return to *my* world
My duvet is sprinkled with pretty colours
Into which spirals are curled.

Rosie Pearce (9)
Colneis County Junior School

CAKE TO STOMACH

I'm eating my smooth, creamy, rich,
succulent, delicious, chocolate cake.
It enters my mouth-watering saliva-filled
mouth where my jaws start to chew,
munch and grind the cake between
my white, pearly-shaped teeth.
As I swallow the marble-sized piece
of cake, my large red sensor-tasting
tongues pushes it to the back of my throat
and into my elasticated, elongated
tubing gullet where it squeezes and
pushes the marble-sized piece of cake
into my acidic, watery, bubbling,
stretching, liquidising stomach!

Stevie Davison (10)
Colneis County Junior School

RIVER TO THE SEA

Calmly how the river moves
In ripples, till suddenly one
Enormous storm, *splash!*
Pulls the river to the sea.
Swiftly it flows, yet gently
And shimmers in the darkness
Like diamonds in the moonlit sky.

Hannah Purser (9)
Colneis County Junior School

LONELINESS

I feel like a kangaroo with no jump,
I feel like a tiger with no stripes,
I feel like a bird with no wings,
I think it's loneliness.

I feel like an elephant with no trunk,
I feel like a cat with no whiskers,
I feel like a lion with no roar,
I feel like the wind with no breeze,
I think it's loneliness.

I feel that no one likes me,
I feel that no one comes to me,
It is loneliness.

Anna Gillies (10)
Elmsett CE Primary School

FEAR

Spooky, sneaky, soundless, silent,
Fear creeps up me, down me, all around me,
Eek!
Spiders
Spooky, sneaky, soundless silent
Round, around me, always in me, fear,
Oh no!
Egyptian mummies!
Spooky, sneaky, soundless, silent.

Stephen Strudwick (10)
Elmsett CE Primary School

CREEPING NOISE

I hear a creeping noise at night,
It fills me full of fright,
Is it a burglar, broken into the house?
Or maybe it's my brother's pet mouse.

Whatever it is I have to see,
Oh why, oh why, does it have to be me?

I hear that creeping noise again,
Is it going to stop? And if so . . . when?
I'm hiding under my covers now,
I have to get away . . . but how?

Whatever it is I have to see
Oh why, oh why, does it have to be me?

I hear it coming up the stairs,
Is it hoping to catch me unawares?
It's coming through my bedroom door,
Creeping over my toy-ridden floor.

Whatever it is I have to see
Oh why, oh why, does it have to be me?

Crash! Bang! Wallop! Aargh!
It's fallen over my toy car!
I pounce, then down on all fours,
Flashlight on . . .

It's Santa Claus!

Eleanor Pierpoint (11)
Elmsett CE Primary School

FEELING SAD

I'm feeling sad, I don't know why,
I'm feeling sad, I'm about to cry,
I'm feeling sad and quite unhappy,
And that makes me an unhappy chappy.

I'm feeling sad and depressed,
I'm feeling sad and hopeless,
I'm feeling sad and now I'm crying,
I think I know why, my great aunt's dying.

I'm feeling sad, which makes me moody,
I'm feeling sad so I speak very rudely,
I'm feeling sad and upset,
I'm taking my dog to be put down at the vet's.

I'm feeling sad, my dog's just died,
I'm feeling sad, his body's inside,
I'm feeling sad and cheerless,
I'm definitely not completely fearless.

I'm feeling sad, I'm not getting better,
I'm feeling sad, I just got a letter,
I'm feeling sad, because it said,
Tonight my mum will die in bed.

Alice Holland (9)
Elmsett CE Primary School

THE SPOTTED DINOSAUR

One grey day I looked up and saw,
A great big spotted dinosaur!
Out of the wood the great beast came
I walked right up and asked his name.

He told me 'Al, and I can fly,
I'll take you high up in the sky.'
Off the ground we flew away!
Couldn't manage it and fell in the hay.

We tried again and took of quick
We went so fast I felt quite sick
After a while we were high off the ground
I had a good chance to look around

Then as we began to dive
I said 'Cor it's good to be alive.'
I didn't hear what Al said
Because I woke up in my bed!

Ben Duff (9)
Holbrook Primary School

CHASE

Little green men speeding by
Going past the traffic lights
Here come the police
After them
Off the little men go again
In a cloud of smoke.

Martyn Bass (9)
Holbrook Primary School

NOISES AT WORK

Factory

Bang goes the stamping press,
Hiss goes the lathe,
Whistle go the workers as they work,
Rumble goes the conveyor belt,
Hmm, go the motors,
Ding goes the bell for time to stop work,
And everyone goes home.

Office

Tick goes the clock,
Tap goes the typewriter,
Rustle goes the paper,
Chat go the workers in the office,
Ring goes the telephone,
Whirr goes the PC,
And everyone goes home.

Building Site

Saw goes the saw,
Drip goes the tap,
Shout go the builders,
Scratch goes the shovel against a stone,
Scrape go the bricks,
Swoosh goes the lorryload of sand,
And everyone goes home.

Robert Carey (10)
Holbrook Primary School

FOOTBALL

Saturday's here, up I sit
Get my boot bag, pack my kit
Need my breakfast so I'm fit
Then sit down and rest a bit.

Walked to the field
Got onto the grass
Started the match
And made the first pass.

The ball went to Theo
Then went to Dan
Who passed it to me
And onwards I ran

I dribbled the ball
Right past defence
And got a great goal
The cheers were immense.

Back to the centre
I ran with a beam
But then I woke up
It was only a dream.

James Brown (9)
Holbrook Primary School

COLOURED CATS

My cat is yellow
My cat is white
My cat is as black as night
My cat is purple
My cat is pink
My cat makes others wink

My cat is bluey
My cat is green
My cat is cool, have you seen?
My cat is orange
My cat is red
My cat likes to eat brown bread.

Charlotte Gant (10)
Holbrook Primary School

PETS

Dogs, dogs, what's the point in them
They're really cuddly and sweet.
OK, OK, I suppose they're cute
But they're messy and mine's definitely not neat.

Hamsters, hamster, why do we have them?
Well, they're small and cuddly and soft,
Yeah, yeah, they are really funny
But it wasn't when we lost mine in the loft!

Rabbits, rabbits, what do they do?
They're so sweet with their two floppy ears,
OK, OK, I love them too,
I've had mine for about three years.

Cats, cats, what are they for?
Well, of course, they're friendly and sparky maybe.
Yeah, yeah, I suppose you're right again
They're sweet and cuddly like the rest can be!

Pets, pets, I think they're all cool
Especially dogs, hamsters,
Rabbits, cats and the rest,
They *rule!*

Rosanne Hiles (10)
Holbrook Primary School

THE ALIEN POEM

Ten little aliens running around on Mars.
One hit a mine,
Then there were nine.

Nine little aliens had to catch a rocket.
One was very late,
Then there were eight.

Eight little aliens racing around in space.
One flew to Heaven,
Then there were seven.

Seven little aliens visiting Neptune.
One got in a fix,
Then there were six.

Six little aliens swimming around on Pluto.
One did a dive,
Then there were five.

Five little aliens waiting for a trip to Saturn
One was too poor,
Then there were four.

Four little aliens walking on the Moon.
One went in for tea,
Then there were three.

Three little aliens playing in outer space.
One went to the loo,
Then there were two.

Two little aliens playing with a time machine.
Suddenly one was gone,
Then there was one.

One little alien fighting with a space bug.
He tried to be a hero.
Then there was *zero*.

Matthew Parrish (9)
Holbrook Primary School

MY FAVOURITE COUSIN

Eleanor's my favourite cousin,
She's only just turned one,
Even though she's very small,
We still have lots of fun.

Even though she's very small
She still makes lots of noise.
Although she cannot crawl yet
She can play with all her toys.

She loves to go to the playing field
To play on lots of things.
She loves to watch me playing
Especially on the swings.

She loves her scrumptious dinner
It goes down a treat.
It ends up mostly on her face,
But I think she's very sweet.

James Loveland (9)
Holbrook Primary School

THE UNDER-SEA ARGUMENT

There was an old dolphin called
Harold,
Who had a wife called Sally Young.
They fought and they fought
Altogether,
So something just had to be done.

A parrot was called in from China,
He said 'What on earth's going on?'
They worked it out with no problem,
And that is the end of my song.

Fabia Conington (9)
Holbrook Primary School

THE SPOTTED DINOSAUR

I sat in my egg
And it started to crack
And when I got out my mum called me Steg
Then I started to eat my first leaf

I've got a green spot
And a purple head
With an orange and violet and white bot
And also a blue and white tail

I took my first walk
But I still fell over
And it took me ages to try and talk
Then it did finally come out

I ate a big leaf
It filled my tummy
I have the shortest but thickest white teeth
That are dying to grind down some grub.

Jessie Keeble (9)
Holbrook Primary School

THE POWER

Behind the tiger's mouth
Is the power of its cold, stone-like teeth,
Behind the power of its teeth
Is the power of its red, hot, fiery eyes,
Behind the power of its eyes
Is the power of its camouflage,
Behind the power of its camouflage
Is the power of its tenderness towards its cubs,
Behind the power of its tenderness
Is the power of its nature,
Behind the power of its nature
Is the power of nothing.

Thomas Stroud (10)
Holbrook Primary School

SNAKES

There are lots of different types of snakes
Which live in ponds, rivers, or even lakes
They have lots of different enemies
Including beautiful birds, gliding in the breeze
Sometimes it depends on what they eat
It could be a little field mouse eating honey and wheat
Although they have all these funny features
They are still the prey of some strange creatures
They could be ancestors of the dinosaurs
Who had long teeth and funny claws
They have lots of other prey
It could even be an owl hiding in the hay
Yet in some cases they are ferocious
And their eating habits may be atrocious
But they have lots of different patterns
Which you think look good with rubies and satin
But this is not what they're good for
They have rights, is that the explanation you're looking for?

Paul Barker (10)
Holbrook Primary School

INSIDE THE LION'S EYE

Inside the lion's eye the prey of a deer
Inside the lion's eye a bite in the throat
Inside the lion's eye a nose of No Fear
Inside the lion's eye the fisherman in his boat.

Inside the lion's eye the fearless furry mane
Inside the lion's eye the sharp claws
Inside the lion's eye the hot, burning flames
Inside the lion's eye the soft paws.

Inside the lion's eye all its blood and fur
Inside the lion's eye his killing pride
Inside the lion's eye its soft and gentle purr
But most of all
Inside the lion's eye its instinct to hide.

Matthew Longson (10)
Holbrook Primary School

JUNGLE RUN

I was walking in the jungle
When I saw a bunny
That was in a bungle
But it looked quite funny.

I carried on walking
I saw a hawk
That was talking
But it looked like a stork.

My shoes were battered
I saw an orang-utan
And he chatted and chatted
And he had a lovely suntan.

I won't forget today
I had a really great day
But I had to pay
Hopefully I'll come back some way.

It turned out to be a dream
But it was fun
I had a scream
And now I have done.

Poppy Fisk (10)
Holbrook Primary School

A DAY'S RIDING

Saturday morning,
When I am able,
I like to go down,
To Hill Farm Stable.

Horses to feed,
And stables to clean out,
It's really hard work,
And there is no doubt.

Louise and Elaine,
Show us the way,
To take out the muck,
And feed them the hay.

It's really good fun,
When we go on a hack,
An hour has gone
By the time we get back.

We usually go,
Close to Pinn Mill,
Over the fields,
And down a big hill.

Cantering and trotting,
Are really quite fast,
Trees and hedges,
Go whizzing past.

When I get home,
I slump in the chair,
I'm really worn out,
With straw in my hair.

Kate Barker (10)
Holbrook Primary School

MY BROTHER IS A PAIN

My brother is a pain,
He's quite insane,
He plays on the computer,
Again and again.

> He wakes up in the morning,
> Still yawning,
> While typing on the keyboard,
> He's still snoring.

> He comes home from school,
> Makes his bag fall,
> He goes onto the Internet,
> To surf for the intellects.

He's completely obsessed,
I think he's possessed,
Oh no!
He's turning into the Internet.

Charlotte Moore (10)
Holbrook Primary School

DOGS IN THE PARK

Greyhounds racing,
Spaniels chasing,
Labradors playing,
Great Danes laying,
Jack Russells barking,
German shepherds marking.
Red setters meeting,
Poodles eating.

Katie Milligan (10)
Holbrook Primary School

THE BEAUTY OF NATURE

The beauty of nature is a wondrous sight
So behold it now in true delight
The beauty of nature is a wonderful thing
So listen to the birds who so merrily sing.

The snowy owl in a green oak tree
The tiny bugs you can hardly see
The digging mole going underground
A mouse creeping without a sound.

The swan gliding gracefully across a lake
The slither and hiss of a passing snake
The pounce of a lion to catch some prey
The elegant swimming of a manta ray.

The animals I have mentioned are but a few
To ensure their survival they need help from you
It's your duty you understand
To save them for the next generation's land.

Daniel Stebbings (10)
Holbrook Primary School

FIREWORKS

Fireworks are purple
Fireworks are green
Fireworks are orange
Some are aquamarine.

Fireworks explode
Fireworks go pop
Fireworks can bang
Some fireworks don't stop.

They brighten the sky
Like huge shining lights.
They're lovely and beautiful
Wonderful sights.

Fiona Tunbridge (9)
Holbrook Primary School

CREATURE FEATURES

Cats prowling
Birds squawking
Monkeys howling
Parrots talking

Peckers tapping
Buffaloes barging
Crocs snapping
Rhinos charging

Hyenas laughing
Leopards spotting
Antelopes calving
Carcasses rotting

Zebras crossing
Baboons bossing
Snakes slithering
Spiders' deadly sting

Watch where you walk
Try not to talk
Animals everywhere
Look about, beware!

Theodore Vass (10)
Holbrook Primary School

ELEGY OF A SPACEMAN

Floating in space
Not knowing your place.
Past Saturn's coloured rings,
Comets, and other strange things.

Floating, feeling weightless
Now passing Uranus.
Not knowing your place
In the middle of dark space.

Humming a tune
While passing Neptune.
Floating through space
Now guessing your place.

Floating around Mars
In the light of the stars.
Now knowing your place
In the vastness of space.

Mark Frost (9)
Holbrook Primary School

COLOURS OF THE RAINBOW

Red as a rose
Blue as the sea
Green as the grass
Yellow as can be

Black as soot
Pink as a pig
White as the snow
Brown as a fig

Silver as a trophy
Orange as the sun
Maroon as a brick
Gold as a gun

Grey as the clouds
Lime as a pear
Purple as a plum
And blonde as a hare.

Alex Christensen (9)
Holbrook Primary School

AT THE SEASIDE

Seagulls flying
Children playing
Donkeys neighing
Green flags swaying

Grandads sleeping
Crabs creeping
Ice cream melting
Spades digging

People swimming
Windbreaks flapping
Candyfloss sticking

Lifeboats zooming
Punch and Judy amusing
Piers creaking
Waves are splashing

The seaside is exciting.

Amy Swallow (9)
Holbrook Primary School

HENRY

Henry, my lovely old English sheep dog
Is warm and cuddly to have.

He gallops around with huge feet like clogs
All hairy and white like an old pair of gloves.

He has two beady eyes, one blue and one brown
And he acts like a funny old clown.

His bark is very deep
And he sleeps in a big heap.

I wouldn't sell him for a million pounds,
He is the best out of any hounds.

They say a dog is a man's best friend,
Well Henry's mine until the end.

Bethany Thrower (10)
Holbrook Primary School

MY PET SPIDER

My pet spider lived in a bin,
In my bathroom so I called her Lynne.
At first she was scary because she was hairy,
So I became just a little bit weary.
She had long legs with beady eyes
And so I decided to feed her flies.
She made a web where she went to bed,
So I made her eight slippers and coloured them red.
The bin got smelly when she met her friend 'Ned',
So my mum chucked it out and both spiders were *dead!*

Stephanie Brazil (9)
Holbrook Primary School

THIS IS THE KEY

This is the key to the village.
In the village there is a road.
On the road there is a house.
In the house there is a room.
In the room there is a TV.
On the TV there is a face
On the face is a fly.

Zachary Powell (8)
Hollesley Primary School

THIS IS THE KEY

This is the key to the dungeon
In the dungeon is darkness
In that darkness is a shadow
Behind the shadow is a person
On that person is a sad face.

Rosie Daniell (7)
Hollesley Primary School

THIS IS THE KEY

This is the key to the castle
In that castle is a big room.
In the room is a dungeon.
In the dungeon is a chest.
In the chest is some treasure.

Henry Kember (8)
Hollesley Primary School

THIS IS THE KEY

This is the key that fits the castle
In that castle there is a room
In that room there is a door
Through that door there is an orchard
In that orchard there is a tree
In that tree there is a chest
In that chest there is a box
In that box there is a purse
In that purse there is a coin
With that coin there is a note
On that note there is a message
On that message it says . . .

Rachel Pipe (7)
Hollesley Primary School

THIS IS THE KEY

This is the key that fits the castle
In the castle there is a table
On that table there is a set of drawers
In that set of drawers there is a chest
In that chest there is a box
In the box there is a coin
If you open the coin there is a bright jewel
On the bright jewel there is a face with mad eyes.

Ryan Whitney (7)
Hollesley Primary School

THIS IS THE KEY

This is the key to an orchard
In the orchard there is a castle
In the castle there is a flight of stairs
Up the stairs there is a room
In the room there is a treasure chest
In the treasure chest there is a box
In the box there is a bag
In the bag there are some gold
          and silver coins.

Sophie Sly (8)
Hollesley Primary School

THIS IS THE KEY

This is the key to the house
In the house is a room
In the room is a cot
In the cot there is a chest
In that chest is a box
In the box there is a purse
In the wonderful purse is a necklace
With little silver dots on.

Amy Churchyard (9)
Hollesley Primary School

FROM THE BACK OF THE CAR

Here I sit at the back of the car,
Watching vehicles go by,
Some zooming,
Some rushing,
Some accelerating,
Some racing,
And that's all I think.
As I keep watching I see other things,
Rabbits, hopping round in circles,
Signs saying
'Zoo one mile'
'School ahead' and other things.
Braking.
Perhaps we're nearly there.

Ellie Rogers (8)
Ipswich Preparatory School

THE CAMEL

Yes, I remember long ago
When I travelled miles just to find a crying baby.
Such a screamer!
It was me who was dragged
From the cold outdoors to an even colder barn.
It was my hay they put in the manger.
It was me who accidentally swished my tail
And made the wise men drop their gifts.
Too many people in that place.
I could not bear him
Getting all the attention!

Rebecca Mulcahy (9)
Ipswich Preparatory School

FROM THE BACK OF THE CAR

Here I sit at the back of the car,
Sheep munching madly at the grass,
Watching owl's eyes sneaking at night,
Lorries carrying fuel for Tesco's,
Cows brown, black and white strolling to a new space,
Rabbits hopping round the pigs,
Golden corn waving in the wind gently
Pigeon droppings landing on your car
Cones red and white nearly everywhere
Signs saying 'Give Way' to the cars,
Fields taking up space for lucky animals,
Boys yawning in the back of a passing car,
Sick bowls passing to the back of the car.
Slowing down.
Here we are.

Hannah Jeffery (8)
Ipswich Preparatory School

YOU!

Your brain is the size of an elephant,
You are nearly bald,
You would think you didn't have legs,
You cannot even lift a bottle,
You're big and bulgy,
You sink like a rock in the sea,
You run as fast as a turtle.

George Carlton-Brett (7)
Ipswich Preparatory School

THE INNKEEPER

One December night I'm soundly sleeping
When to my inn two guests come creeping.
They beg me, 'Please give us a room till dawn.
This night our baby will be born.'
'My inn is full, but I've a stable
And a manger for a cradle.'
A star shines bright above the barn,
Their child is born away from harm.
Wise men come from lands afar,
They've travelled miles following the star.
Frankincense, gold and myrrh are gifts they bring
To honour this baby king.
Shepherds too call at my inn.
'An angel sent us' - this makes me grin.
But this child is a special baby,
Is he really Jesus Christ?
Well, maybe.

Ben Hills (9)
Ipswich Preparatory School

WILL THERE BE A FUTURE WE LIKE?

Will the gentle manatees
swim in the turquoise seas?
Perhaps crocodiles will go
and dinosaurs resurrect and grow?
Is this what the future holds?

No snow on the south pole,
no petrol for our cars,
shopping by computer,
a huge city built on Mars?
Is this what the future holds?

Forests dying, deserts spreading,
rubbish piles high,
seas growing, planet fading?
Is this what the future holds?

Christian Swan (8)
Ipswich Preparatory School

JOSEPH

Yes, I remember long ago
When our son Jesus was born
In a soft manger.
The long-eared donkey, the woolly sheep
In the fields nearby, sleeping.
It was me who led the donkey
Along those sandy tracks to safe Bethlehem.
I was worried when gathering hay
That the baby would come later than expected.
I put the hay in the manger,
A crib for the baby.
Later with the donkey and sheep resting
Silently in the warm hay,
I held my son with great joy.
I watched the shepherds kneeling in prayer
Beside the manger where Jesus lay.
I watched Mary clutching carefully
The gifts of the kind wise men.
To think that I was the father
Of a very special king,
God's very own son.
No one could take that away from me.

James Williams (9)
Ipswich Preparatory School

MARY

Yes, I remember long ago
When my darling Jesus, our first born,
Came into the beautiful Earth
That God the Almighty had made.
I wept with joy,
Wept with joy,
Wept with joy.
Humble Joseph was standing over me
He was weeping too.
It was me who brought little Jesus into the world
And I was feeding him milk.
Jesus hugged me gently.
I, the mother of the son of God,
Came out of the stable
One darkening dusk
To see that big, beautiful, magical shining star.
I wept for joy,
I wept for joy,
I wept for joy.
'Oh, you are a darling, my sweet!' said I.
The very next day three kings
Knocked at the stable door
And gave him lovely gifts.
'Oh, I do love you, my darling, my sweet!' said I
And Joseph said the same!

Charlotte Robinson (9)
Ipswich Preparatory School

THE KING

Yes, I remember long ago
When we three kings brought
Frankincense, gold and myrrh
And I was plodding,
Plodding,
Plodding along on my camel.
We were following the golden, magically shining
Huge star.
It was me who gave him the gold
It was me who gave him my cloak to warm his body,
As I was giving,
Giving,
Giving gold to the newborn king.

Yes, I remember long ago,
When we three kings came plodding,
Plodding,
Plodding on our big, fat camels
When an angel told us
To follow the biggest star in the sky.
It was me who rocked him gently
To cheer him up from crying his eyes out.
It was me who gave him the crown of a king
As I was rocking,
Rocking,
Rocking the newborn king.

Oliver Weller (9)
Ipswich Preparatory School

THE SHEEP

Yes, I remember long ago,
When we made that long journey,
That one afar,
Making progress all the time
Following angel Gabriel's golden star.
And I was cold,
Cold,
Cold as an icicle.
We found the ancient inn where we had been led
Where Jesus Christ had been born.
He was lying in a tattered manger.
Our shepherd knelt down low to pray
When three wise men entered the inn
And I was bleating,
Bleating,
Bleating with joy.
One king with gold, another with myrrh
And the final one with frankincense.
But I was bleating,
Bleating,
Bleating with joy.

George Rendall (9)
Ipswich Preparatory School

WHAT WILL THE FUTURE HOLD?

What will the future hold?
Will school be more exciting?
Will we travel by silver micro-scooter
With double parking in the playground?

What will the future hold?
Will everyone carry a super laptop
And a funky mobile phone?
Will clever robots rule our homes?

What will the future hold?
Will our beautiful forests still be standing?
Will our pretty meadows still be green?
Will pollution be at an end?

What will the future hold?
Will my children see the fierce tiger
And the gentle panda
Or will they be extinct?

What will the future hold?

Elizabeth McLachlan (8)
Ipswich Preparatory School

THE STAR

Yes, I remember long ago
On that first Christmas.
I was the star
Twinkling in the sky
Outside an old stable.
I twinkled.
Brighter than a burning red torch,
I spread a golden light with silver shining brightness.
I shone and made baby Jesus smile with joy.
I was shining golden sparks
And lighting up the spooky, dark and lonely night.
I was bright,
I was bright with unbelievable light
When Jesus cried deeply
I cheered him up.
Star! Star! Star!
I was light and beautiful.
Star! Star! Star!

Timmy Yung (9)
Ipswich Preparatory School

WILL THERE BE A FUTURE WE LIKE?

Will snowdrops covered in sparkling frost
Still glitter on the icy ground
During long winter seasons?

Will juicy red berries
Call to merry berry pickers
From fat green bushes?

Will there be
Fresh air to breathe
Which will fill our gasping lungs?

Will sparkling reservoirs
Still gently cool
Beautiful nature?

Will there be
Long bamboo shoots
For pandas to greedily gnaw?

Will there be
A sparkling Aries
For the midnight sky?

Will those things
Still exist
When I'm grown up?

Olivia Lewis (8)
Ipswich Preparatory School

FROM THE BACK OF THE CAR

Here I sit at the back of the car,
Fields flashing by like a blurring picture,
Sheep munching at the grass,
Cows parading, marching across the field.

Orange car approaching slowly and flashing by,
Sign saying one mile to our house,
Favourite sight appearing now,
Passing by,
Now you see it,
Now you don't.

Alexander Mitchell (9)
Ipswich Preparatory School

WILL THERE BE A FUTURE WE LIKE?

Will aliens
From Andromeda
Invade us?

Will the sea
Still be dived in
By fish?

Will the ozone
Be made stronger
By humans?

Will the cane
Be reintroduced
To schools?

Will snails
Still leave
Slimy tracks?

How much
Of the world
Will be left?

William Birkbeck-Martin (8)
Ipswich Preparatory School

Will There Be A Future We Like?

Will Ipswich still be at the top
Or will they drop
To Division One?

Where will I live
When I am a man
In England or Japan?

What will we eat
Boring old vegetables
Or tasty red meat?

What about the weather
When we are old
Will it be warm or cold?

Will we still live on Earth
Or use shiny jet cars
In our new home on Mars?

Joshua Godfrey (9)
Ipswich Preparatory School

The Donkey

Yes, I remember long ago
When I went to the old rustic stable
And I was stomping,
Stomping,
Stomping,
While ripping and pulling the leaves off the trees
And being whipped by kings.
It was me who gave the leaves for Jesus to keep warm with
And then was gently stroked,
Stroked,
Stroked.

Yes, I remember long ago
When that baby was crying,
Crying,
Crying
And I was sleepy,
Sleepy,
Sleepy
And I was braying,
Braying,
Braying a sweet lullaby.

Iain Reynolds (9)
Ipswich Preparatory School

THE MOUSE

Yes, I remember long ago
When God's son was born.
I was scrambling,
Scrambling,
Scrambling through the hole
In the wall.
God's son, the mighty Jesus, was sleeping
Quietly in the manger.
In a stable crowded with big animals
I was scrambling,
Scrambling,
Scrambling through the hole
In the wall.
Jesus was sleeping in the manger
With my amazingly long tail
Swaying one side to the other
Slowly.

Edward Messent (8)
Ipswich Preparatory School

THE DONKEY

Yes, I remember long ago
When I went into that old, dull stable
And I was braying my sweet song;
While Jesus was crying, crying, crying his eyes out
And Mary, his mother, worked harder than ever.
It was me who saw him in the manger.
It was me who carried, yes carried God's only son,
Braying my sweet song.

Yes, I remember long ago
When Joseph and Mary were sitting down smiling
That first ever Christmas.
I was sleeping, sleeping, sleeping in the hay,
While the old shepherds came,
Watching and worshipping their newborn king.
I just slept and slept all through the joy.

Yes, I remember long ago,
When the brave kings followed
The shining, twinkling, bright star
And I was staring, staring, staring at the newborn baby,
While they presented their gifts
And the gold was shining
The myrrh was bright
And the frankincense had no darkness.

It was me who told them
He was a baby
And I was staring, staring, staring at him
And braying my sweet song.
But I still wanted my manger back.

Ahrandeep Aujla (8)
Ipswich Preparatory School

THE INNKEEPER'S DOG

Yes, I remember long ago.
I was only a puppy then,
Barking and lapping my clean water.
I was sniffing,
Sniffing,
Sniffing for danger.
While Mary was cuddling
And Joseph was embracing
It was me who alerted the innkeeper
When baby Jesus cried a lot
Under the starry night,
As I was sniffing,
Sniffing,
Sniffing for danger
When humans asked for quiet.

Yes, I remember long ago
On that first Christmas
Barking and lapping my clean water.
I was sniffing,
Sniffing,
Sniffing for danger.
While Mary was hugging,
Joseph was kissing.
It was me who kept the baby king happy
By running around barking,
As I was sniffing,
Sniffing,
Sniffing for danger.

Ben Manning (9)
Ipswich Preparatory School

FROM THE BACK OF THE CAR

Here I sit at the back of the car,
Rabbits hopping like mad in squares,
Friesian and Jersey cows racing to the milk shed,
Aeroplanes gliding high in the air,
Flies striding over the mud-splattered windows,
Horses galloping far and wide
Brothers arguing loudly behind
Exhausts belching smoke everywhere,
Pedestrians chatting as they cross the road.

Charles Davis (8)
Ipswich Preparatory School

A STORM AT SEA

The lashing, crashing sea's ahead,
The clouded black dark sky,
The cold and stormy wind above,
The dragons fire high.

The captain calls out 'Land ahoy,'
Then 'Only sea' he wails,
The crew are tipped all over the place
And call out 'Pull the sails!'

The sea calms down a little bit,
But still the ship is rocking,
The tide comes in and they go home,
The gallant ship is left alone . . .

Sophie Stokes (10)
Martlesham Beacon Hill Primary School

THE HORSE STEALERS

I was violently pushed into a dark and dingy trailer
We were jostling down a rough, uneven and potholed track
That's when, without warning, the accident took place
The trailer uncontrollably turned over.

There I lay twisting and turning and whinnying for help
Beads of sweat trickled down my face but nobody came to my aid
Suddenly loud sirens came buzzing down the track
My eardrums were bursting with the noise
The horse stealers were arrested
I was reunited with my real owners
Now I am loved, cared for, and the happiest horse in the world.

Jennifer Bickers (10)
Martlesham Beacon Hill Primary School

BLUE WHALE

He is as wide as ten double-decker buses
He is as long as two high schools.
He is king of the ocean.
The king summons up his royal dolphins
To glide solemnly through the water.
Sadly. Lonely.
As the praising crowd cheer off
          on the sunset beach.

Abigail Savoy (9)
Martlesham Beacon Hill Primary School

MOUSE IN THE WOODS

Nowhere to run.
Nowhere to hide.
The soft echo of paws thumping in the night's black grass.
Owl hooting in the scabby tree.
Slight crunching sounds of a little hedgehog scurrying.
In the night's sky, dawn is breaking.

Jennifer Thompson (8)
Martlesham Beacon Hill Primary School

HOW TO MAKE A DRAGON

First take two rubies from the centre of the earth
and take the juice of midnight to enlarge them into eyes.

Next for the scaly skin, scrumple a thousand pieces of paper
and soak them in the green marshes of marshland
for its striking colour.

For its breath, squeeze the sourness of a lemon
and whisk it up with a breeze of wind.

For its speed, take the shimmering tail of a shooting star.

To make its curved claws, take some moon dust from a sickle moon.

Then for its viciousness, take the anger of a wasp
and mix it with a tornado's fury.

Last of all, take the gummy fingers of a baby
and mix the goo with lava from an erupting volcano,
glue everything together and *poof!*
A dragon is born.

Ivan Hunter Gordon (11)
Orwell Park School

How To Make A Bumblebee

Take an iceberg from the Arctic ocean and slice two blades
From the sides to make the bumblebee's wings.

For the skin, peel the stripes of a tiger
And stick them to the body of an acorn with tree sap.

For the eyes, take a million mirrors and cut out of them
Pentagons with the blade of a purple diamond the size of
The scale of a goldfish.
Then stick them all together with the cobweb of a
Black widow spider covered in dew and then you have the eyes.

For the legs, stick six sewing needles into the acorn
This also gives the bee its sharp and painful temper.

Take the pain from a toothache and stick it to a vampire's fang
To make the sting.

Steal the hum of a humming bird and stick it on with honey.

William Stott (11)
Orwell Park School

I Know Someone Who Can

I know someone who gets a constant detention.
I know someone who never grows old.
I know someone who actually likes school.
I know someone who is invisible.
I know someone who can walk on boiling steel.
I know someone who can hold their breath for an hour.
I know someone who is immortal.
I know someone who does not like sweets.
I know someone who reads minds and that person is me.

Adnan Bashir (11)
Orwell Park School

HOW TO MAKE A WOLF

To make a wolf you need . . .

For his skin, capture all the animal kingdom's fur,
mix it together to make the fur as soft as a bird's feather.

For his grey colour, catch a stormy cloud and drain the
colour from it. Mix it with a snowy-white iceberg.

Make his body out of a ball of play doh and shape it
into an oval.

For his tail, get some curved leaves, stick them together
with honeydew and pin them to the body.

Make his eyes from two green emeralds from a mystery
cave.

For his nose, capture a night colour and pour it onto a
Ping-pong ball.

Make his ears out of sharp pointed paper hats.

Then form his head from an island mixed with the brains
of dragons, dogs and humans all placed in the head.

Then for his voice, collect it from a giant's mouth
and make a howl from a microphone so it echoes.

Make him run as fast as lightning, speeding past trees,
rivers and seas.

His beauty is as great as a goddess.

Lois Hunt (11)
Orwell Park School

HOW TO MAKE A FIREWORK

To make a firework you will need to:
Capture a trickle of a rainbow for the colour effect.
For the firework's boldness, get a squint of a lion's roar.
Squeeze a crocodile for its crackly laugh that makes the crackly effect.
Collect two whole armour sets for its roughness
and crush it into millions of tiny pieces.
Snatch a ton of lava from an angry volcano to make the
firework's anger.
Dip these into a roaring storm to make the firework's howl.
Drag an angry giant and stir him into the roughness of the lion
to make the firework whiz up to the stars.
You will be left with the best firework in the *world!*

Heather Moate (10)
Orwell Park School

HOW TO MAKE A RAINBOW

Take the tail of a comet and curve it like a Sumo wrestler's bottom,
then tie it to the Earth with a spider's diamond lace.
Crush in the seven moons of Saturn and sprinkle it on the comet's tail
to make it sparkle.
For red, squeeze the blood from a tiger.
For orange, take the magma of a volcano.
For yellow, take the shavings of an old man's stick.
For green, take the skin of a Boomslang.
For blue, take the blood of a prince
and for indigo and violet, take a flower picked in the Himalayas.

Hugh Creasy (11)
Orwell Park School

HOW TO MAKE A GIANT

Take the weight of a Sumo wrestler and stretch it into a ball.
Take the strength of a crane and sprinkle it onto the ball
and it will form into the template of a giant.
Take twenty books from the National History Museum
and put them in the head.
Take two handfuls of blazing fire and put them on the head for eyes.
Suck out the roughness of gravel, split it in half and then wrap it
up in two plastic sheets.
Mould them onto the arms for hands.
Take the sting of a bee and bind it with 500 egg yolks.
Cut the mixture in half and put them on the legs for feet.
Take the green of broccoli and mould into teeth.
Take the smell from a fart and put it in the mouth for breath.
Take the size from a mountain and add it to the almost body.
Take the temper from a storm and plant it in the head.
For clothes, take the scrap metal from a car factory
and mould it all over him.

Congratulations! You have successfully made a giant.

Edmund Compton (10)
Orwell Park School

HOW TO MAKE A CROCODILE

Get the teeth from a saw,
Get an emerald from the regions of hell for its green eyes.
Get the spikes of a cactus for its horny back.
Capture the anger from a raging storm for its cruel nature.
Get the jaws from a bear trap for its clamping mouth.
Get the tail length from a bridge.
Get the strength from a thousand stallions.
Glue it all together with molten lava from a raging volcano.

Oliver Reeves (10)
Orwell Park School

HOW TO MAKE A THUNDERSTORM

Drain the black from the dark night sky and mix it with the smoke
of a dragon with a bad temper, to make the cloud.

Get a four hundred metre lead up to the cloud and plug it into
a nuclear power station to make the lightning.

To make the falling rain, get a bucket and catch the tears
of an upset giant, then mix it with some sort of chemical
from a chemistry lab to make acid rain.
(You don't have to do this but it makes it more exciting)

To make the anger of the storm, suck the temper out of the sea.
If this does not work you could always try working up your teacher.

Then to finish it all off, take a tusk of an elephant
and mix them all together in a big black bucket and *bang!*

Mark Mckechnie (11)
Orwell Park School

HOW TO MAKE A TRAIN

Take the scary scream of one million serpents
And mix it in with the roar of dragons in an angry fury.
Then take the steam of a single factory chimney
And a fire that has just had cold water put on it.
For step number three, take the dim light of the biggest storm
In the world and mix it with three new batteries,
So as not to make it too dark.
Then take the power of the waves knocking down a sandcastle
And mix it with the strength of Atlas, the man who lifts the skies.
Then put this into an elephant's belly and watch the elephant's body
Turn into a long snaking steam train.

Alexander Bond (11)
Orwell Park School

HOW TO MAKE A PERFECT PERSON

To make a perfect person you need . . .
For her skin a fresh glass of coconut milk.
Her red lips are quilted from a velvet cushion.

Her smile is taken from a ray of sunshine,
Her beauty is as pure as a mountain spring
Running through the hills.

Her nature is plucked from a rooster strutting
And a tiger prowling,
Her love is a blooming flower picked from a breezy meadow.

Her laugh is a gentle squall but it catches distant minds,
Her generosity is whipped from Orion's belt of stars.

Her brains are made of an eagle's cunningness,
Her figure is curved and sleek as a panther.

Her imagination swirls in multicoloured rainbow stripes,
Her hair is a sweeping velvet curtain.
This perfect person is a woman!

Elizabeth Barrett (11)
Orwell Park School

AWESOME AUTUMN

Autumn is a special time of year
With changes there and changes here.
Conkers appear, smooth and brown,
Leaves turn red and fall to the ground.
Nuts and berries, fallen seeds,
Beautiful sunsets glowing through the trees.
Birds fly south to retreat from the cold,
Pearls of dew like silver and gold!

Steven Everson (10)
Ranelagh Primary School

AUTUMNATIC

An eyeball with a dull brown iris staring
Autumnatically at you,
A brown, crinkly, emerging
Veined hand
Denying death, which is
Autumnatically
Inevitable,
An 'F' shaped letter standing
Autumnatically
For finished life.
The change has
Begun!

Roomi Miah (11)
Ranelagh Primary School

EGYPTIAN POEM

Rameses' head rolled over the sand,
Sphinxes laugh while pharaohs dance,
Pyramids built by thousands of men,
King Tut's tomb lost in the den,
Carter feels what he might seek,
The smell of the tomb just reeked.

While fair is foul and foul is fair,
Egyptians laugh and babies stare,
Objects that we are to keep,
Spirits of the Egyptians will never sleep.

Natasha Taylor (11)
Ranelagh Primary School

THE SPHINX

In Egypt lies the Sphinx
Every day and night he winx
Looking at the pyramids
I wonder what he thinx
Boiling in the sun
Still there is the rain
Wishing and wishing
That the pharaohs were there again
Going back to sleep with memories to keep
Of long ago
When he gazed upon the pharaohs.

Gemma Bennington (10)
Ranelagh Primary School

MATHS QUIZ

I am sitting on my chair feeling so glum
Trying to work out a hard maths sum.
My teeth are chattering
I have a wobbly knee
It's like taking a voyage over the sea,
But wait a minute I know this sum
The answer is 241
Now my voyage I think is done.
Wait a minute the answer's wrong!
No need to worry I've got to be strong
The answer is 541,
Now my voyage is really done.

Robert Lappin (9)
St George's Preparatory School, Southwold

POOH STICKS

Broken from a chestnut tree,
Carried to a bridge,
Dropped into the flowing water.
Weeds are clogging my path,
I'm in danger of orange sharks.
I hear a voice cry
'I've won, my stick's gone the furthest.'
It's a dream come true!
Lilies are blocking my path
I become entangled,
They're strangling me
I'm struggling for my life,
I'm free,
I'm on my own ship,
Until I get to the sea.

Daisy Jellicoe (10)
St George's Preparatory School, Southwold

WALKING TO MY DESTINY

The burning sun beating down on my neck,
Droplets of salty water trickling down my face,
Brown sugar lumps crumbling underneath my soggy toes,
Seagulls swooping down in front of me,
Stringy grass dancing in the wind,
Candyfloss bubbling in the sky,
Frothy sea whooshing against the dry sand,
Leaving behind a trail of popping seaweed,
Chasing a kite in the wind,
Leaving behind the perfect paradise.

Hannah Bugg (10)
St George's Preparatory School, Southwold

DREAM JOURNEY

Every night I have the same dream . . .
I am on a ship sailing miles out to sea
The turquoise water lapping at the ship's hull
A slight breeze tickling my skin.
Looking far out to sea,
I spot a beautiful island
Where the ship will land
But there is no port or harbour,
Just soft sand, white and silky.
The ship's voyage across the sea
Has come to an end at last
Leaving past and present behind,
But beginning a new life, a fresh start . . .
I turn around to thank the ship, but it has gone,
Sailing into the deep sea mist.
I find myself on my favourite perch
A rock jutting high over the waves.
Thinking of my long voyage across the sea . . .
Now all is silent
Only the faint sound coming from below,
Water crawling up the beach
Like a crab . . .
I sit and watch the sun go down.

Katie Howl (9)
St George's Preparatory School, Southwold

THE DRAGONFLY

I fly across the lake,
My reflection following me.
The quiet buzzing of my wings,
Fizzing in my ears.
As I glide across the water,
The sun beams in my beady eyes.

I drift up to the reeds,
A gnat is flying past,
I catch it in my basket-like legs.
My large wings whizzing up and down,
I'm the devil's darning needle,
The mosquito hawk too!

Emily Girling (10)
St George's Preparatory School, Southwold

STRAY ON A VOYAGE

All my life, I have been passed around.
Nobody cared,
I didn't even have a name until I came into care.
I have been passed around like a package never opened,
My whole life has been a voyage,
A voyage from one home to another until I move on.
It's like I am always on a ship,
I have been to every island, each as horrible as the last.
My first voyage was to a home . . .
It smelt old and dull,
It felt lifeless.
The children would tease me,
'Mary-Anne,' they would call,
I hated it, I hated everything about my life,
My life full of voyages.
But now, back on the boat to who knows where,
I hate this life,
Nowhere to go,
Nowhere to stay,
For I am a stray.

Frith Janes (10)
St George's Preparatory School, Southwold

DOWN TO A WATER WORLD

I fall asleep
Spinning, falling
Into a deep sleep,
Splash!
I land in cold water,
A waterfall.
I plunge into the water below,
My eyes all blurred with water,
A whirlpool.
Spinning,
Round, round,
Slowly,
I stop spinning.
My eyes fall open,
My dreamland disappears.

Amy Hall (10)
St George's Preparatory School, Southwold

DREAMBOAT

When you fall asleep . . .
The dreamboat skims through your brain.
It glides through your sea of thoughts.
It's as graceful as a swan.
Through the depth of enchanting dreams,
There's death and pain!
This is the place where darkness reigns
Evil, wicked nightmares scurry
Anger and sadness attack the ship!
The dreamboat drifts past in tatters and ruins.
It drifts past and dissolves in the deep sea mist.

Stephanie Salter (10)
St George's Preparatory School, Southwold

SPACESHIP

It travels through the dark and empty space,
Travelling from planet to planet,
No one can see it,
Because it is camouflaged with black.
It is an alien's ship,
Because it fires meteors down onto us
And because it has a skeleton flag,
It means that they are pure evil.
As it dodges in and out of the planets,
It makes a loud clattering, banging and whooshing sound.
It will destroy anything in its path.
It travels through each galaxy.
Once this spaceship has been destroyed,
What will be left of our space?

Taryna Ormerod (10)
St George's Preparatory School, Southwold

SPACE VOYAGE

As I drift away and fall asleep
There's a hush, not even a peep.
I'm on an aircraft going to Mars
I look above and see the stars.
The ship is floating
Like a ship that is free
As the silence ebbs through me
Like the tide of the sea.

Laura Green (10)
St George's Preparatory School, Southwold

THE THEME PARK ADVENTURE

My adventure ride is going to start,
I have butterflies in my tummy.
My tummy is turning inside out.
Water's splashing in my face.
There are huge waves coming over my rubber ring.
I'm turning round and round,
I am all wet and sticky,
I am coming to the end.
There is an elephant spraying water on my face.
My adventure has finished and I want to do it all over again.

Rio Ives (10)
St George's Preparatory School, Southwold

MY CAT'S TRAVELS

I have a cat called Mouser
Her fur is very long
She prowls around the garden
Disturbing the birds' song
I have a cat called Mouser
She hunts for food at night
In the day she hides away
And sleeps out of our sight
I have a cat called Mouser
She sometimes goes away
She comes back much, much later
Sometimes another day!

Isobel Puddifoot (10)
St George's Preparatory School, Southwold

TO BE A FROZEN RAINDROP

I wonder what it's like to be a frozen raindrop
To be hanging off a frosted tile on a very snowy roof
To be crystal clear all over
Then the sun would come out
And I would be part of a puddle
But then what would I be?
I wouldn't be an animal
I wouldn't be a machine
Do you know what I'd be?
Have you ever been a frozen raindrop?

Hannah Pickess (10)
St George's Preparatory School, Southwold

I'D LIKE TO BE A PIRATE

I'd like to be a pirate
Riding on the sea
A parrot on my shoulder
And a crooked knee.
Looking for the treasure
Up and down, across.
Ah ha I've found it
It's in this rusty box.
I open up with a golden key
My eyes are beaming at what I do see
Gold, silver and bronze
Rubies, diamonds
It's a pirate's *treasure!*

Isabella Singleton (10)
St George's Preparatory School, Southwold

THE DREAM

I board the ship
For a long, dangerous trip
To a faraway place
Deep, deep into space.
I look at my crew
A rabbit, a shrew
A cow and a dog
And a black and white frog.
As we fly oh so fast
Looking as the land goes past
Fields of grass so bright and green
And flowers that you've never seen.
Boulder fields so dull and grey
And fish chewing at some hay
Treetops with their snowy peaks
And clouds of mist so cold and bleak
And through the mist a storm's about to rise
To a great, almighty size
When with a sudden shake
I wake.

Alex Wetten (10)
St George's Preparatory School, Southwold

THE DIVER'S JOURNEY

I dived into the deep blue sea
I swam rapidly through all the tropical fish.
My eyes searched for all the beautiful things that were around me.
I saw a red little crab scuttling at the bottom of the sea.
Soon I was face to face with a black man-eating shark
I looked around and it was clear water
I rushed back to the outside world.

Jade Annett (10)
St Helen's Primary School, Ipswich

The Floor's View Of A Journey

Carpet is a hairy wolf skin
Rough as splintery wood
Feet . . . vast deserts
Lift a body
The size of Africa
Onto this wooden floor.

Feet the size of a school
Rise and fall
'Til they reach the table
A giant grinning face
Staring at *my* ant face!
Paper, soft and deadly
Hand picks it up
Vaster than a chocolate bar
Each step is longer
Down
Down
Squash!
I have been squashed!

Elizabeth Johnson (9)
St Helen's Primary School, Ipswich

The Brave Wooden Ship

Bravely the wooden ship was sailing on the blue, calm sea.
Steadily the sea splashed gently across the ship.
Turning the afternoon,
The sea roared, destroying like an angry lion.
Rapidly the sea splashed into the lion's mouth.
Steadily the wooden ship climbed its way back up
And landed on dry land.

Natalya Edwards (9)
St Helen's Primary School, Ipswich

MY JOURNEY IN THE SKY

In this life of mine
I have no cares,
The journey I shall take,
Will fulfil my longing for freedom.

Soaring high above the world,
With an untimely passion.
As I spiral the silver shrouded clouds,
I feel a heavenly sense of belonging.

The ripples from the wind
Creep up on me, ruffling my feathers
Like a well-rehearsed Swan Lake.

My hopeful destination,
Will be down south
Nearer the hotter climates.

Should my wings ever be clipped,
My journey would be over.
But for now,
I shall continue
Like a jet plane leaving a translucent marking in the sky!

Harriet Joseph (10)
St Helen's Primary School, Ipswich

ORCA

Ebony eyes,
Misty nightshade,
Smooth glider,
Echo sender,
Gentle giant,
Deep murmerer,
Plankton diner.

Black and white bairn,
Gliding along beside,
Watchful,
Wary, roused.

Harriet Rose Robinson (10)
St Helen's Primary School, Ipswich

DOWN IMAGINARY LANE

Images all around
Most of them make no sense
A few resembling a dog
Good heavens!
It's him!
My imagination!
In a lime green suit and topaz top hat
Number 1 on his shirt
Amazing!
Weird!
Really cool!
He winks at me
'Yo!' he says, asking me to follow.

Leading me down an unknown alley
A cat shivers
Now Imagination leans towards my ear and tells me
'Eager as you may be, don't be a fool and follow me
for I am going to a wonderful place,
with apple pie trees and marshmallow lawns.
You cannot enter for this place does not exist for the human race.
You need to be imaginary to see it!'

Thomas Russell (10)
St Helen's Primary School, Ipswich

THE WHALE POOL

As the sea ripples in front of me I glide through the azure water.
I am as snug as anything, with a thick coat of blubber covering me.
Getting deeper and feeling more pressure I glide onwards
I call to my friends waiting their reply but I hear nothing
Up and up I shall go and sing to the moon
I shall dive in and out of the waves
I drift on but everything seems like a lifetime to me
It's getting dark but I can see
The fog is making my vision blurred.
Passing through the harbour, the light shines brightly
The stars twinkle in the moonlit sky.
Reflections like ivory-laced pillows lie staring upwards.
I will get there some day
To the whale pool to meet my friends
My friends and me.

Jessica Cartmel (10)
St Helen's Primary School, Ipswich

JOURNEY THROUGH LIFE

The journey through life is the greatest leap
An uneasy shuffle
Voyage through life's seas my be endless
The journey through life may be brief
All the seasons running wild
While winter passes, summer sleeps
Autumn sheds its crispy leaves
Spring will see blossoms, flowers and wealth
All this happens but of course
Sweet life will still go on.

Peter Randall (11)
St Helen's Primary School, Ipswich

FOREST FERN

Going on a trek
Through leaves and trees.
Getting very irate with a puny giant.

Forsaken your friends
Disastrous ending to your uncles!

Seek to find the frankness
About cherish.

Vigorous guides you
To destiny.

Destiny guides you
To joyousness.

A life full lugubriousness
Wanting to terminate.

Ending up obtaining.

Peter William Hazelwood (9)
St Helen's Primary School, Ipswich

MOONLIGHT'S DELIGHT

Up, up through starry lemon-lights
Sky
flash, glisten, twinkle, gleaming
Stars
flying past the galaxy
Mars! Jupiter!
Galore!
Unmindful sky
- that's the moonlight's delight.

Natasha Curtis (10)
St Helen's Primary School, Ipswich

A Trip To South Africa

The writer of this poem
Is going on a journey
As brave as can be
Going to have lion for tea.

As strong as an ox
As clever as a boffin
As hard as a rock
He's swimming to South Africa.

The writer of this poem
Joshua Goodwin is his name
He's going to have fun
In the South African jungle.

He is going really deep
Where no one's been before
He's going to be as swift as a monkey
Who loves his cup of tea.

Joshua Goodwin (10)
St Helen's Primary School, Ipswich

Sky-Glider

Slowly swooping bird
Up, up, going far away
Like a vast eagle.

Gliding across black hole
Starry, silky moonlit sky
Glowing in the dark.

Sky is brightening up
Sun is starting to come up now
Morning has begun!

Emma Smith (10)
St Helen's Primary School, Ipswich

ROLLER COASTER RIDE

Wait for passengers,
depart from station,
goes the little train.
Up 'n down,
left 'n right
goes the little train.
        Up the hill,
        loop the loop,
        goes the little train.
Zoom! Whoosh!
Splish 'n splash,
goes the little train.
Snap, snap,
take a photo,
of the little train.
        Hold on tight,
        down the hill,
        goes the little train.
Oh no the ride has ended,
pull into the station little train,
but don't fear it will all happen again
for my little train!

Lisa Cousens (10)
St Helen's Primary School, Ipswich

THE GALLEON GOBBLER!

For very ship there's a storm
for every twist there's a turn
for every storm there's a thousand
white horses galloping on the surface.

But then as I glide through the smoky cloud-coloured ocean
I can see ahead of me a bright light
with a long red and white pole underneath.
The light is becoming closer and closer . . .

For once there are no smoky clouds,
no white horses and there are no galleon gobblers!

I'm there!

Rosalind Borwick (10)
St Helen's Primary School, Ipswich

TIDYING MY ROOM

I am mad, moaning,
I am screaming, upset,
I am annoyed, shouting,
I kick, hit,
I am rough, bullying,
I am hurtful, harming,
I am angry, frustrated,
With my work done,
I am pleased, happy,
I remember, my money,
Oops,
I've made a mess,
Again!

Kirscha Brown-Powell (9)
St Helen's Primary School, Ipswich

THE BRAVE LITTLE SHIP

There was a little brave wooden ship
That sailed out on a beautiful sunny day
On a calm crystal sea.
The waves in the sea started to get a bit rougher
And the wind was like a lion blowing and roaring.
Clouds were getting darker and darker,
Clouds were getting closer and closer.
The boat started to sink into a mouth of a roaring lion
But the ship didn't taste nice
So the lion spat the ship out onto the shore.

Georgina Lamb (10)
St Helen's Primary School, Ipswich

THE BULLET SHIP

Bullet ship races against
Raging water lions,
Man-hunter
Crew-drowner!

Bullet ship soars through
Water trap,
Ship-cruncher
Cursed ocean!

Bullet ship tries to escape
Shark-breeder
Murderous splash
Crunch!

Is this nature's revenge?

Alastair Gilles (9)
St Helen's Primary School, Ipswich

TORNADO

There's danger in the air
so you'd better take care 'cus Tornado is back
he's gonna' attack, ain't nobody gonna' be meaner
your dreams will be gone but he don't care
he'll just carry on, he'll always be there
he never gives up or runs away,
'cus the wrecking tornado is here to stay.
Thundering across town
destroying anything in sight,
he spells trouble with a capital 'T'.
So don't go takin' no liberty.
He's a tornado,
you can always find him,
it's just losing him that's hard!

David Looney (10)
St Helen's Primary School, Ipswich

THE STEAM TRAIN!

Faster than rockets, faster than lightning.
Screaming and scratching the train rattles along.
The smell of the coal, the clank of the wheels.
Out of the window the world goes by.
Mountains are a rocky death trap.
The river is golden, as clear as the air.
The fields are being harvested by the reaper.
Faster than anything, now it's all *gone!*

Kyle Parmenter (11)
St Helen's Primary School, Ipswich

I LOVE OLD PLACES

I love old places,
Where the roofs of churches
Are fallen in,
And only the walls are left standing.

The silence rings in my ears,
Only birdsong breaks the morning air,
It wakes me up
From my silent daydream.

The cold nips at my fingers,
The isolation is paradise,
I wander through arches,
My curiosity knowing no bounds.

To others wind is cold,
To me it is like hot sun,
And the icy rain
Is joy to my heart.

The wet grass, the stone,
The quartz sparkling in the sun,
As if the granite had thousands
Of disco lights fused into it.

I love the fog,
No knowing where you're going,
In the rolling thick blanket,
Like waves breaking on the shore.

I love old places,
Where the roofs of churches
Are fallen in,
And only the walls are left standing.

Edward Leach (11)
St Margaret's CE Primary School, Ipswich

I LOVE CREEPY PLACES

I love creepy places,
Where cobwebs hang from the ceiling,
And my heart beats fast,
While nasty noises screech.

I love creepy places,
When the wind flows through your hair,
And sends a chill
Down your spine.

I love creepy places,
Where ghosts and ghouls hide,
And shadows creep round corners,
To really scare you.

I love creepy places,
Where things go bump
And crash,
And I jump in fright.

I love creepy places,
Where floorboards creak,
As I tread lightly,
With soft footsteps.

I love creepy places,
But no one will go in,
Except me of course,
'Cause I love it in there.

Joseph Richardson (10)
St Margaret's CE Primary School, Ipswich

SNOWY PLACES

I love snowy places
Where I can ski down fast,
Where I wish and whoosh
Past foggy people.

I love cold snow
As it hits my face like wind,
I see my skis like fast cars
When they go in the snow.

I go back up the drag lift
And go just as speedy,
The snow, as soft as silk,
Where I dance my way down.

I love my heart racing
With the beat of people falling.
I fall down in soft snow
Where my face gets as pale as pale.

I go down quick as light,
Never trying to slow down.
My heart is pumping like my face,
And never stops a race.

The snow twinkles like the sun
Twinkling in my eyes,
I know what to do
With my eyes like the stars.

I love snowy places,
Where I can ski down fast,
Past blurred and foggy people,
This is where I love.

James Bigley (11)
St Margaret's CE Primary School, Ipswich

I LOVE ISOLATED PLACES

I love isolated places
Where nothing moves except me
Silence
Not even a mouse makes a noise.

No traffic
No hatred
Just the wilderness and me
Not a care in the world.

No hassle
Just peace and quiet
I can throw stones in the river
So they skim across the water.

I don't have to do anything but lie,
Lie in the sun
With the cool breeze in my hair
No work to be done.

No bullies
No war
No slavery
No trouble.

Jack Burfield (10)
St Margaret's CE Primary School, Ipswich

A MYSTERY HOLDER

A mystery holder,
A life scolder.

A creature eater,
An animal beater.

A strong water winder,
A vicious storm finder.

A mermaid seater,
A pretty world deeper.

Rebekah Irving (10)
St Margaret's CE Primary School, Ipswich

I LOVE MUDDY PLACES

I love muddy places,
At a football field,
Where the players
Have trampled everywhere.

I love the atmosphere,
All the fans chanting,
The away team being boo-ed off,
And the winning team cheering.

I love the feeling,
Of squelching in the mud,
Hearing the squelch,
And having to wipe the muck off.

I love the smell,
Of all the burgers,
And the smoke,
And best of all, the mud.

I love thinking about it,
Days later, having to pick mud off
My boots after leaving it
For days and days.

Alistair Lang (10)
St Margaret's CE Primary School, Ipswich

I LOVE SNOWY PLACES

I like snowy places
Where the crisp snow falls on my face
I can feel the icy feeling
Which spreads around me.

I like watching the snow fall from the sky
And seeing everything white
I like to see my cat
Ski across the ice.

I like to see and feel the snow
On my warm glove
I can see the snow
All around me at night.

I like the wintry atmosphere
And how it glides through me
I like to jump around and throw
Snowballs at my sister.

Dominic Isles (11)
St Margaret's CE Primary School, Ipswich

SILENT PLACES

I love silent places
Where it's dark
And I can hear my heart
Beating *boom, boom!*

When everything is still
And I can hear a pin drop,
I love it in my room
When it is silent.

Where I can think all day
Alone on the floor
With the carpet rubbing
On the backs of my legs.

When I am silent
I can do what I want.
Dream is what I like to do most.
I love sitting in silent places.

Holly Etheridge (11)
St Margaret's CE Primary School, Ipswich

SANDY PLACES

I love sandy places
Where the sea clashes
Against the rocks
And the sand swirls around.

When I go and
Swim in the warm sea
And I see the fishes
Bounce up and down.

Eventually I get out
And wrap up warm
Then I breathe in
The smell of the sea.

At last the day
Is nearly over
'Cause I saw the
Sun set behind the sea.

Rachel Player (10)
St Margaret's CE Primary School, Ipswich

I LOVE SLIPPERY PLACES

I love slippery places,
Where people slip over,
Whilst enjoying themselves,
On the very cold ice.

In other cold places,
Birds are having great fun,
Chasing each other,
On the very slippery ice.

On a freezing cold day,
I can slip over on frozen lakes,
And even try and skate,
But I know I will slip and fall over.

David Fewkes (11)
St Margaret's CE Primary School, Ipswich

A GRASS MUNCHER

A grass muncher
A daisy cruncher

A tail swisher
A lazy wisher

A sleepy slicker
A long licker

A milk carrier
A plant marrier

A lonely weeper
A soft sleeper.

Kirsty Topping-Green (11)
St Margaret's CE Primary School, Ipswich

THE SECRET GARDEN

The air was like frost in the darkness,
No light was to be seen anywhere.
Nothing could be felt,
Except the slight touch of cold and icy air.

As the trees' silhouettes became fainter,
Nothing could be seen.
Except for the branches
Swaying on the old oak trees.

No flowers were to be seen in sight,
No light had ever shone,
All that was there was an empty space.
But where had everything gone?

Tiny weeds grew,
The grass began to spread,
Little birds sang,
Flowers grew in their bed.

Buds became flowers,
With petals soft like velvet,
They grew and grew into towers,
Growing taller every minute.

But who would look after this garden?
Was it a mystery to all mankind?
Did anyone know its secret?
What would happen and who would mind?

Sophie Temple (10)
St Mary's RC Primary School, Lowestoft

FIRE AND FLAMES

Fire burning in the house,
In the pitch-black night.
Right on time the firemen came
Each with hoses as long as snakes.

A light came on in the houses at midnight,
No more sleep for the whole long street.
Night and flames but no more sleep.

Flames are misty in the burning house,
London's not burning on that night.
A burn of fire and no more sleep,
Morning strikes and the fire engine's gone.
But let's hope there's not another fire,
Not a single person in sight.
The house is wrecked,
But it looks like a dump.

Sebastian Lock (9)
St Mary's RC Primary School, Lowestoft

LIVING ROOM

TV a giant, pitched dark hole,
Chair as soft as a cushion,
Walls like barbed wire,
That locks me in tight.

The floor all messy,
We tidy it up,
When it is clean,
It looks like a maze,
But when it is littered,
We think it's like a zoo.

When I need to go out,
I'm always watching TV,
When it's turned off,
I think it's on.
I go off to the shops,
To buy a newspaper,
Then I come back home,
Then I come back home.

James Taylor (10)
St Mary's RC Primary School, Lowestoft

OVER PEBBLES

Over pebbles, over stones.
You see all the beautiful shapes,
That lie there on the golden sand.

Over pebbles, over stones.
Wherever you go you see them,
Some of them are peculiar
And some of them are the same.

Over pebbles, over stones.
Whenever you try to hide,
They will be right behind you.

Over pebbles, over stones.
If you are sad,
Look at them,
It makes you feel much happier.

Over pebbles, over stones.
If you take one home,
And wish, your wish will
Come true.

Georgia Yeaman (9)
St Mary's RC Primary School, Lowestoft

THE DREADED CASTLE

T is for the treasure hidden beneath the castle,
H is for the haunting phantom moaning and crying,
E is for King Edward's spectre roaming about.

D is for dreaded mayhem in the castle,
R is for the raiders raiding the castle,
E is for the magical elves that scuttle about,
A is for the angels that sing all night long,
D is for the dead of night, the knights come charging in,
E is for the endless noise that rings out of it,
D is for the dancers prancing around.

C is for the creepers creeping about the castle,
A is for the ants that crawl around the castle,
S is for the poltergeists that moan and mumble around the fort,
T is for the trolls that scuttle beneath the knights' legs,
L is for the landlord's daughter's spook rapping at the door,
E is for King Edward's ghost!

That is how you spell the *dreaded castle!*

Daisha Anne Lewis (9)
St Mary's RC Primary School, Lowestoft

THE SEA

The sea is raging with the wind and the sand of the beach.
Islands are trampled over by big, white sea horses.
Waves are raging in the storm with fish,
Whirled round and round, as if in a whirlpool.

People would not come in for a swim,
Sharks would dodge rough waves.
Dolphins were jumping in and out of the water.
Islands, towns and cities were overlapped by the rough waves.

It was the worst storm ever to be seen.
The rain clattered onto the sea and the thunder clashed,
And the lightning crackled.
Suddenly there was a peak of light,
Which was the sun starting to come out.

The storm was over!

Chelsea Long (9)
St Mary's RC Primary School, Lowestoft

THE GRAVEYARD

Full moon in the sky,
Screams of horror came from inside the haunted church.
The clock was striking twelve,
In the distance a wolf howls into the night.
The souls of the dead rise,
Going to haunt the living.

The wind blusters around the graves,
Waking the living,
Crumbling parts of gravestones,
Waving around with the whistling wind.

Stars are in the sky,
Dark clouds float by.
Damp, waterlogged grass.
On the ground there are leaves like cornflakes.
The strange sounds are becoming deafening,
Every minute more and more.

The sun is rising,
The souls of the dead are returning,
This is the graveyard,
The haunted graveyard.

Emily Lawrence (9)
St Mary's RC Primary School, Lowestoft

ONE CLOUD

There are many clouds in the sky
But there is only one I know.
It's like a pillow on my bed.
And like a roll of candyfloss
That melts by heat.
It floats up high and guides me.
Through the night
This cloud watches over me.

This cloud is out all the time
In summer, in the winter and all
Four seasons.
When it snows and when it
Rains you'll always see this cloud
But a raindrop will never fall
From it.
Even though it's lonely and very sad
It will never shed a tear.
I only know this cloud.

Jessie Meenan (9)
St Mary's RC Primary School, Lowestoft

GIRAFFE

The giraffe is a mammal whose neck is high, as high as the Eiffel tower.
Legs as big as a skyscraper, a hundred metres tall.
Body like the sea, endless.
Large black spots like oil stains.
Head, the funny shape of a horse, with a long sticky tongue.
Clutching the leaves ten at a time, curling his tongue back up.
Tail is the same as a dog's.

Helen Moran (9)
St Mary's RC Primary School, Lowestoft